KT-539-408

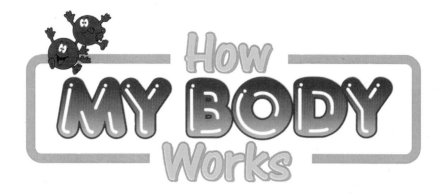

# How
# MY BODY
# Works

## The
## Teeth

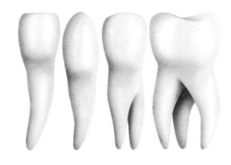

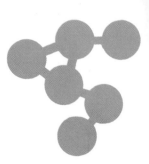

# Teeth

## Getting to know your teeth – and your dentist

You need teeth to chop up food into small pieces so that it can be easily swallowed and sent down to the stomach. Without teeth, you wouldn't be able to eat at all. But even though they're so important, most of us don't look after our teeth properly, and only think about them when we have to go the dentist.

About 98 percent of adults living in the West have tooth decay or gum disease. There are lots of reasons why our teeth can get damaged, such as eating foods that are too hard, or not cleaning our teeth properly. But the main cause of tooth decay is eating foods that contain too much sugar in them, because sugar makes teeth rot.

Most people worry about going to the dentist, but there is really nothing to be scared of. Dentists use painkillers, so you won't even feel the dreaded drill!

Dentists also have very sophisticated equipment, which helps them to do all sorts of amazing things. They can not only give you fillings to mend the holes in your teeth, they can make new teeth for you if your old ones fall out!

*There's no end to our wise Professor's skills. Here he's acting as a dentist, and looks all set to use the drill. He knows that with an anaesthetic nothing is going to hurt the patient.*

The Professor directs the body's defence system. He and Metro, his lieutenant, work to protect your body. Globus and his team of red blood cells need protection as they travel the body delivering oxygen. So Captain Courageous, chief of the white corpuscles and his friends Ace and Corpo cruise around the body attacking their enemies Virulus, the virus and Toxicus, the bacterium.

# CONTENTS

| Incisor | Canine | Premolar | Molar |

# A tooth for every job

Teeth have different shapes because of the different jobs they have to do. You have three types of teeth on each jaw – incisors, canines and molars.

● **Incisors** are at the front of your mouth. They have flat sharp edges because they have to cut into food as you bite it.

● **Canines** are fang-like teeth at the front of your mouth. They hold on to tough food like meat and tear it apart, which is why they're long and pointed.

● **Premolars** and **molars** are at the sides and back of your mouth. They grind food to make it easier to swallow.

*Have you guessed already where the word 'odontologist' comes from? It derives from the Greek. 'Odontos' meaning tooth and the ending '-ologist' always refers to 'the one who knows' – the scientist.*

# Baring your teeth!

Each tooth has two main parts: the crown and the root.

● The **crown** sticks up out of the gum, and is the part of the tooth you can see.

● The **root** is the part that's buried in the gum. Incisors and canines have only one root; premolars have two and molars have three.

● Roots sit in special cavities in the jaw bone called **tooth sockets** or **alveoli**. A bone-like layer of tissue called cementum 'glues' the roots into place and stops your teeth from moving around when you eat.

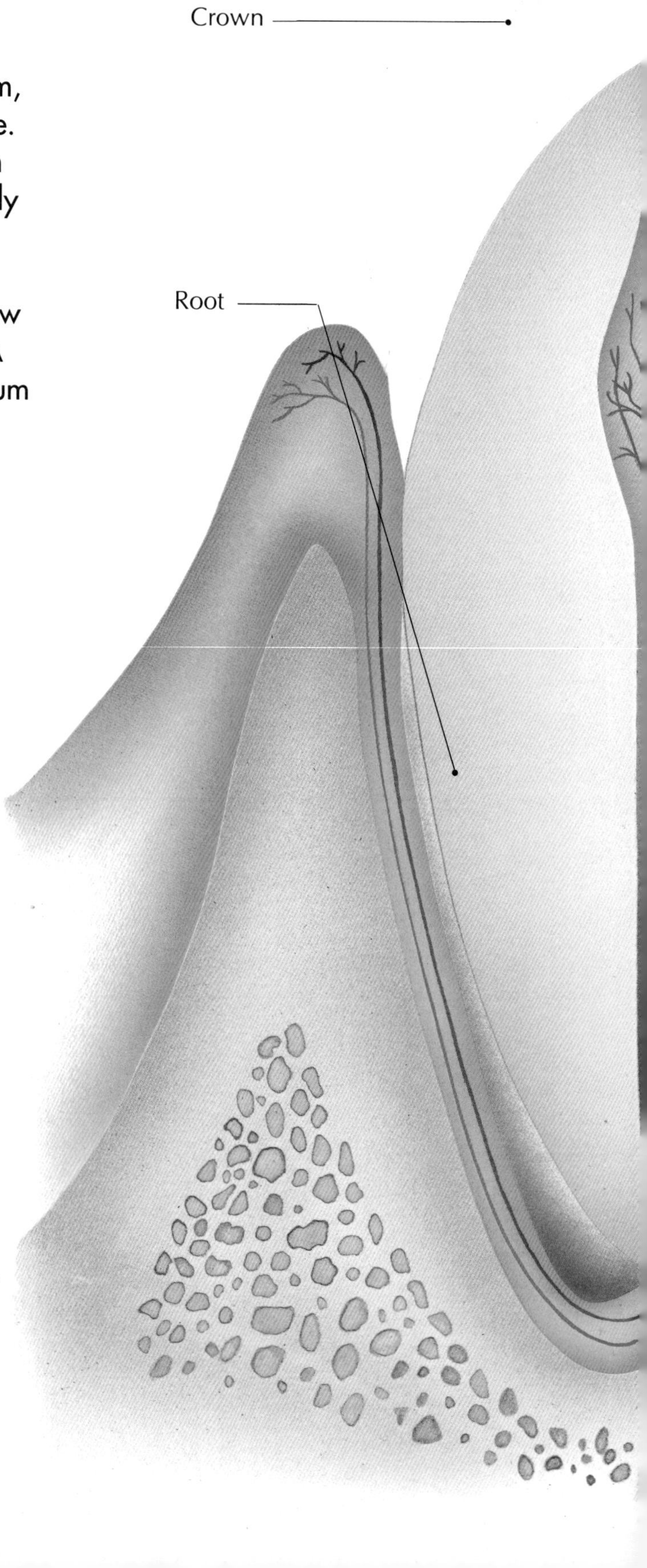

Crown ——————————————•

Root

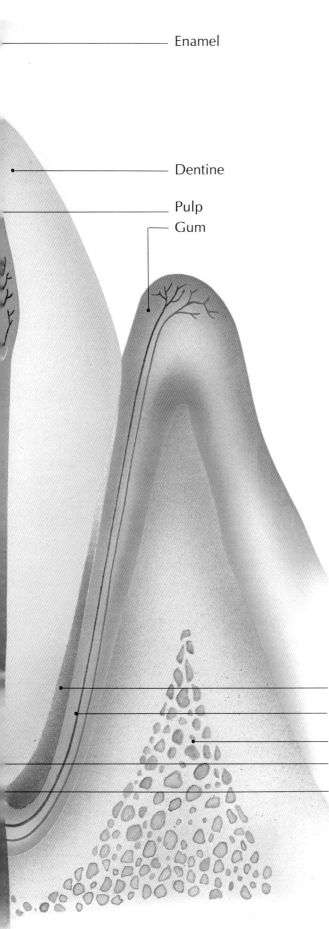

Enamel

Dentine

Pulp

Gum

Cementum

Alveolus

Jaw bone

Nerve

Capillaries

# What's in a tooth?

This picture shows what a tooth looks like when it's cut through the middle. As you can see, each tooth has two outer layers and there's a cavity in the centre.

Starting from the outside, the first layer is enamel. Enamel is the white part of the tooth you can see. It only covers the crown of the tooth because that's the part which is exposed and needs the most protection. Enamel is mostly made up of calcium salts and is the hardest substance in your body. It gives your teeth a strong biting surface and stops them from wearing out.

The second layer is made of ivory, or dentine – a yellowy bone-like substance which makes up most of the crown and root. Like enamel, dentine is made up of calcium salts (70 per cent), but also has ossein, which is found in bone.

The cavity inside is made up of soft tissue called pulp. Pulp contains blood vessels, which supply the tooth with food and oxygen, and nerves, which make the tooth feel pain and temperature.

That's why your teeth sometimes ache when you drink something very cold.

*Toothache happens when you don't look after your teeth properly. Our friend has a bad case and needs the dentist – badly.*

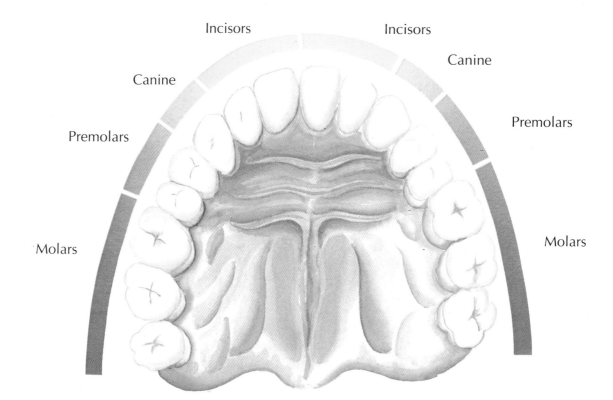

Incisors

Canine

Premolars

Molars

Incisors

Canine

Premolars

Molars

**THE TEETH OF THE UPPER JAW (ADULT)**

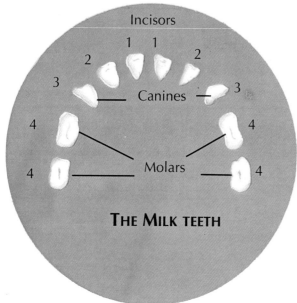

Incisors

1  1

2          2

3              3

Canines

4              4

Molars

4          4

**THE MILK TEETH**

# How many teeth do you have?

The number of teeth you have changes with age. This is because everyone gets two sets of teeth (although no one knows why). The first set, known as baby teeth, or 'milk teeth', is only temporary. It starts to develop when you're a baby and is fully formed by the time you are two years old. A full set of milk teeth has 20 teeth.

At the age of six or seven, you start to lose your milk teeth and get your second, or permanent, teeth. A full set of adult teeth numbers 32. That's 12 more than in your milk teeth, so your jaw has to grow to fit them all in.

*Teething – the process of growing out or 'cutting' teeth – can be a very uncomfortable business. It can make you feel off-colour, and you may not want to eat.*

# DO TEETH GROW?

In human beings, teeth stop growing once they have emerged fully from the gums. But some animals, such as rabbits, have teeth that carry on growing. Have you ever watched a rabbit eating a carrot? If you have, you'll notice that it uses its teeth to scrape off little bits of the carrot at a time. This is called gnawing. A rabbit's teeth are specially made for this because the two front incisors at the top and bottom are very long and curved – ideal for shredding vegetables. This means they can shred food easily. Every time a rabbit gnaws on some food, its two upper front teeth scrape against its two lower ones, and it is this constant scraping which wears the teeth down.

*There's a wide gap between a rabbit's molars and incisors. Scientists reckon that rabbit's teeth keep on growing. If a rabbit's top incisor breaks or falls out, the incisor on the lower jaw grows to fill the space.*

# Something To Chew Over

## How do you chew?

Teeth are there to mash up the food you eat so that it can be easily swallowed and sent down into the stomach. This mashing process is called chewing. Think about how your teeth and jaws move when you're eating, say, a roll.

When you bite the roll, you use your incisors at the front. That's easy if the roll is soft and fresh. But it it isn't, your canines will have to help – they're better suited to biting and tearing because they're pointed. Once the piece of roll is bitten off, your tongue carries it to the molars at the back of your mouth, which start grinding it like a mill. Once the teeth have finished their job, final preparations are made for the food to enter the stomach. Saliva is added by the salivary glands in the

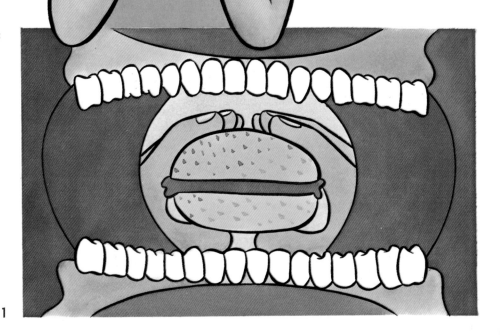

*1. Mmm! This roll looks delicious. So delicious that our friend hasn't given a thought to the hard job his teeth have to do while he's enjoying it.*

1

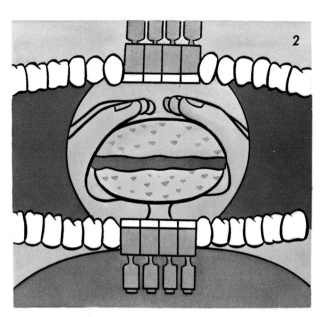

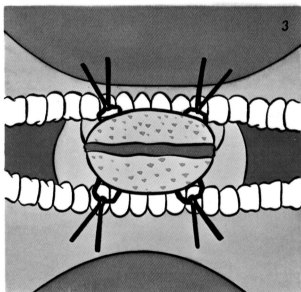

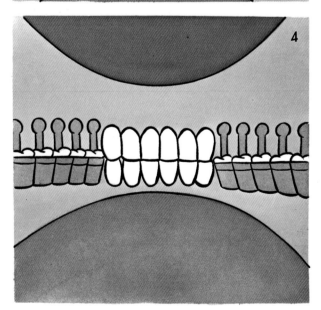

throat, making the food soft and mushy. Then the tongue moves it around into a ball, and pushes it to the back of the throat, ready for swallowing.

How do you chew your food? Everyone does it differently. Many people eat too quickly, take bites that are too big, and then don't chew them for long enough. It's much better to take small bites and chew them properly until your saliva makes them soft and easy to swallow. It's also important to try to chew on both sides of the mouth, otherwise your jaw might develop crookedly.

If you chew properly, your digestive juices will then do their job more easily. Eating too quickly can make you feel bloated and give you indigestion.

So as our friend has probably forgotten, chewing is very important in order to digest food properly. Look at the diagrams to see what happens to his roll when he has decided to eat it.

*2. As the roll enters his mouth, he opens his jaws wide to take the first bite. The incisors (in purple) close like scissors to bite a piece of the roll.*

*3. The pointed canines (in black) grip the roll to hold it in place and rip off a piece as the hands pull what's left of the roll away from the mouth.*

*4. The molars at the sides and back of the mouth (in purple) grind and mash up the food. Saliva is added by the salivary glands above and below the tongue, to make the food wet and mushy and easy to swallow.*

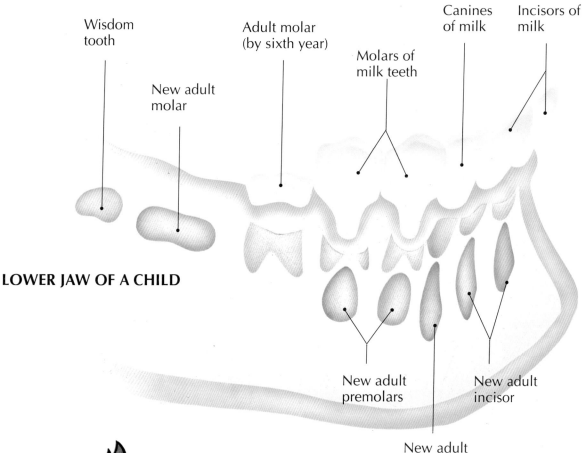

Wisdom tooth

New adult molar

Adult molar (by sixth year)

Molars of milk teeth

Canines of milk

Incisors of milk

**LOWER JAW OF A CHILD**

New adult premolars

New adult incisor

New adult canine

*Babies can't do very much with their first tooth, but it's always a big event for their family and friends.*

# Your first teeth

First teeth, or milk teeth, start developing in babies while they are still in their mother's womb, but don't actually come out until 6-8 months of age. They're fully formed by the time a child is about two. A full set of milk teeth has 20 teeth (10 on top and 10 at the bottom). The first to appear are usually the incisors in the front of your mouth. By the time the set is complete, you will have eight incisors, four canines, and eight molars.

It doesn't really matter how soon or how late milk teeth appear, as long as they're strong and grow in the right place. Sometimes they can be quite far apart. This doesn't mean that they are badly formed – just that the permanent teeth will be bigger than the milk teeth.

At around the age of six, the milk teeth start to feel loose and fall out and permanent teeth begin to grow in their place. Although this can happen at different ages, your milk teeth have usually completely gone by the time you are 14.

Remember though that just because your milk teeth are only temporary, it doesn't mean that you don't need to look after them.

*This is how you look when you lose your first milk tooth and are waiting for your new, adult tooth. Our friend may feel he looks a little silly, but remember: new teeth are a sign of growing up and becoming an adult.*

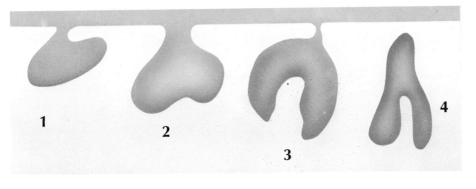

1  2  3  4

## HOW A TOOTH DEVELOPS

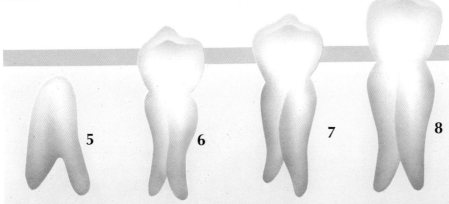

5  6  7  8

*These illustrations show the sequence of how a tooth forms and grows.
Stages 1-4. The root starts to form and grow under the gum.
Stages 5-8. The crown begins to develop, then finally breaks through the gum.*

# JAWS!

Different animals have different types of teeth, depending on what they eat. Plant eaters like horses, which eat grass and hay, don't need canines because they don't eat tough food like meat. They do, however, have three pairs of incisors which act like sharp grass-cutters. They also have six pairs of molars at the back of their mouths which have special pointed ends called 'cusps' to grind delicate bits of grass. In between is a toothless area called the diastema, which is where the bridle fits.

In another plant-eating animal, the elephant, the upper incisors have become amazingly large to form its tusks, which are made of ivory. Although elephants have such large incisors they don't use them for eating – they have another set of teeth for that. But they do need their tusks to tear the bark off trees before they can eat it.

Baleen whales have special teeth called 'barbels'. They don't look like teeth, but are more like horny plates, with ridges. The barbels act like a sieve or a net, which traps the small fish and snails that the whales like to feed on.

*Amazingly, the whale has no teeth. As the whale's huge mouth fills with water, fish and other seafood swim inside. The whale then closes its mouth, and its barbels prevent the trapped animals from escaping.*

Like other plant-eaters, horses have special teeth. To be able to cut and grind their food they have three pairs of incisors at the front and very pointed sharp molars at the back. Although the tusks to the right and left of the elephant's trunk are two giant incisors, the elephant uses another set of teeth inside its mouth for eating. Sadly, many people still hunt elephants for the ivory in their tusks, even though this practice has now been banned.

# Your second teeth

Between the ages of five and ten your milk teeth fall out, one at a time, and are replaced by the larger adult teeth which you will have for the rest of your life. The first adult tooth to come out is usually a molar, which appears at about six years of age. Over the next few years you will get your new incisors, then your canines, premolars and other molars. The full set of adult teeth consists of eight incisors, four canines, eight premolars and 12 molars, but the last four molars, called 'wisdom teeth', don't come out till your late teens or twenties. In many people, wisdom teeth never appear at all, but stay tucked under the gums for ever. This doesn't matter because you don't really need wisdom teeth to eat properly.

Teeth are arranged so that both rows touch and form a strong seal when you close your mouth. The upper row of teeth usually covers the lower row but in some people it's the other way around as you can see in this picture! This bite abnormality is called 'exognathism' or over-bite of the lower jaw.

*'Wisdom teeth' are so called because by the time they appear you are an adult – and are supposedly wise!*

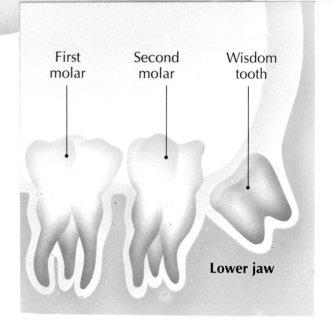

First molar    Second molar    Wisdom tooth

**Lower jaw**

# TEETHING PROBLEMS

In many countries, people use thin pointed sticks called toothpicks for scraping away the bits of food that can get stuck between their teeth. Toothpicks are usually made from wood but they can be made from other things like plastic. They have been used at least since ancient Roman times. In those days, rich people like well-fed Romans would even have had silver toothpicks.

Some people, even then, thought the whole custom was rather impolite. Good manners would have required them to cover their mouth with one hand while using the toothpick, although our friend below doesn't seem too bothered.

Today, we know that using toothpicks can irritate the gum. The best way of caring for your teeth is to use a toothbrush and dental floss.

# Healthy Teeth

## Look after your teeth!

The type of teeth you have is generally inherited from your parents. If they have good teeth, and they looked after them, the chances are that you will too. But there are many things you can do to keep your teeth healthy too. Just stick to the simple rules below

● Avoid all sugary foods and drinks. Eat sugar-free sweets if possible.

● Use dental floss – a length of waxed string – after each meal to remove the bits of food that get stuck in the gaps between your teeth. (Ask your parents to show you how!)

● Try to brush your teeth after every meal or snack. If that's a problem, eat a piece of cheese after each meal (it helps protect the enamel on your teeth) and brush your teeth at least once a day.

'Watch out – sugar's bad for your teeth'

*Sugar is bad for your teeth because it's known to be the main cause of tooth decay. Every time you eat something sweet, the liquid from your food will stick to your teeth. Try sliding your tongue around your teeth – do they feel a bit gluey? This stickiness is caused by something called plaque which makes bacteria. If the stickiness stays, the bacteria make tiny holes in your teeth which get bigger and bigger. Eventually you will have tooth decay – and toothache! Plaque can start to build up just half an hour after eating, so take care of your teeth!*

# Clean your teeth!

Brushing your teeth regularly stops plaque from building up in your teeth and will help protect them from tooth decay. When you were very young, your parents will have cleaned your teeth for you. But from the age of three onwards, the chances are that you'll have been doing them yourself.

You have to be very careful how you clean your teeth. Choose a brush that's not too hard – your dentist is the best person to advise you. Make sure, especially, that you clean between them. If you take care of your teeth properly, they will last you all your life!

*Sometimes you just don't feel like cleaning your teeth. That's only natural, but try to overcome the feeling because looking after your teeth is a favour you owe yourself.*

*At the very least, clean them after breakfast in the morning and when you go to bed at night. Try to drink only water during the night if you wake up – sweet drinks leave deposits on your teeth. If you've got younger brothers or sisters, do them a favour too, and help them to get used to a toothbrush and toothpaste. Once they've got the cleaning habit, they won't break it in a hurry. And that's good for everyone.*

# Watch out – caries is about!

The biggest threat to your teeth is tooth decay, or caries. Caries usually starts betweeen the teeth and in places where the tooth meets the gum.

Every time you chew, small bits of the food you eat get stuck between and on your teeth. If left, this will eventually make plaque – a rough sticky substance you can sometimes feel if you pass the tip

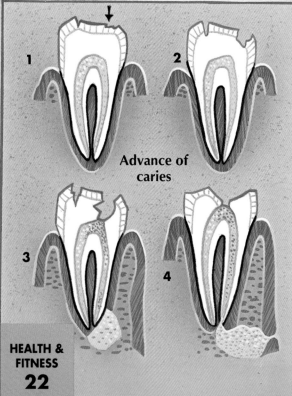

**Advance of caries**

1

2

3

4

*Once caries gets a hold it's virtually impossible to stop. In stages 1 and 2 the caries starts to* *attack the tooth enamel. By 3, pus has begun to form. By 4 there are signs of an abscess.*

of your tongue over your teeth. The bacteria in the plaque feed on sugar in food and make acid, which then starts to eat away at the enamel in your teeth, leaving tiny holes.

If the holes are left, they'll get bigger , and the acids will reach the next layer of your teeth. Eventually, if you don't do anything to remove them, the acids will get into the pulp cavity of your teeth – the 'feeling part' which has nerves. Your tooth will now be very sensitive to hot, cold or very sweet foods, and you will probably get toothache. If your gum is attacked by acid, it will get red and swollen and lose its layer of cementum, which will make your tooth fall out.

Once the holes start to appear in the enamel, the enamel can never grow back. Instead, the holes have to be filled with metal by a dentist. This is why they're called fillings.

*Here you can see the dangerous tooth destroyers at their nasty work. As soon as you feed these evil caries-men with sweets, they go wild, climb all over your teeth, and start attacking them. The more sugar you feed them, the stronger they get, until eventually they might kill your teeth, unless your dentist gets the chance to stop them.*

# F for Fluoride

The best way to avoid caries is to ban sugar from your food as much as possible. But another important way is to use fluoride (which has the chemical symbol F). Medical tests have shown that fluoride hardens the enamel and makes it more resistant to tooth decay. In many countries, fluoride is believed to be so important that it's put in the drinking water so that everyone can get the benefits from it. Sometimes, if the fluoride level in your water supply is very low, your dentist can give you fluoride tablets. But it's much easier to just use a toothpaste that has fluoride in it. Check, next time you buy your toothpaste, that it has the 'fluoride' or 'anti-plaque' on the tube somewhere!

*Fluoride is a chemical compound. But Globina knows that it's not really just one thing, but a mixture of many different substances that you have in small amounts in your dentine, blood and bones.*

Anti-plaque

Dentifresh with fluoride

# Sugar – your teeth's number one enemy !

Sugar encourages the bacteria in your mouth to make acids. These acids attack the enamel and, if left to their own devices, can destroy your teeth, so:

● The more sugar you eat, the more likely you are to have tooth decay. This has been proved all over the world.
Sugar-cane cutters in South America get more tooth decay than other people because of how much sugar cane juice they drink.

● Eskimos only started to get tooth decay in recent years, when they changed to a typical Western diet. Before that, their normal diet of fish kept their teeth healthy.

● It's difficult to ban sugar from your diet completely, but try at least to avoid sugary drinks, and don't eat sugar between meals. Everything helps!

*Sugar is very popular – especially with bacteria! It can provide you with more energy but too much is bad for you. So try not to give in to cravings for sweets. They'll taste delicious today, but tomorrow your teeth could suffer!*

Sugar

Sugar

# How to help

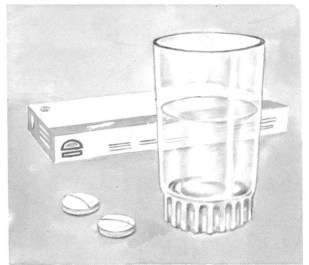

There's nothing worse than toothache, as anyone who has had it knows. You've probably heard your parents or other members of your family complaining about it from time to time. Or perhaps you've even had it yourself.

When you have toothache you will have a throbbing pain in your tooth and the gums around it may get red and swollen. You may even find that your gums are bleeding. If the toothache is really bad you might even have a temperature.

Toothache is usually a sign of tooth decay, and only a dentist will be able to treat the tooth properly. But you can help yourself to get rid of the pain until your appointment by taking aspirin or other pain-killers.

*Never take different kinds of pain-killers at the same time because that can be dangerous. If you want to take something stronger than aspirin, take care. And never take more than the recommended dose. Many pain-killers can only be had on prescription, and under the supervision of your family doctor.*

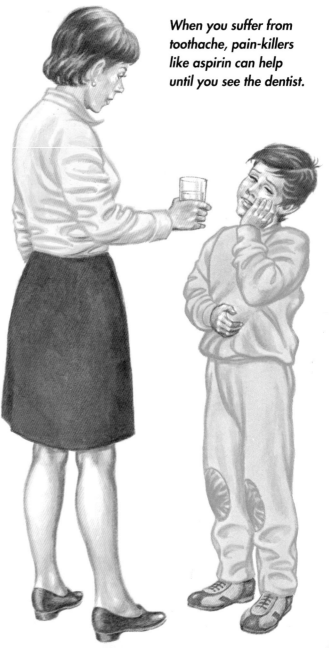

*When you suffer from toothache, pain-killers like aspirin can help until you see the dentist.*

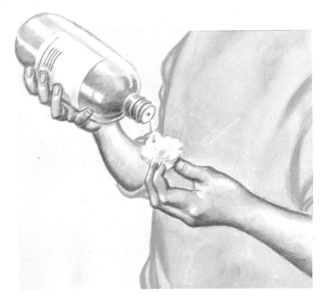

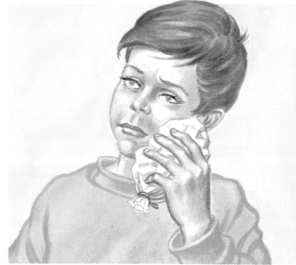

*An often used home remedy for toothache is clove oil. Pour a few drops of the oil on to a*

*piece of cotton wool, and then place the cotton wool on the infected tooth.*

*Ice helps to deaden pain as well and an ice pack held to your cheek can relieve toothache*

*for a short period of time. The cold from the ice should numb the painful area.*

A tried and tested home remedy for toothache is clove oil, which you should be able to buy at your local chemist. Put a few drops of the oil on a piece of cotton wool, then put the cotton wool on to the aching tooth. The clove oil will soon make the pain better, but be careful because it's very strong. Don't let the oil touch your gum or tongue, because it can sometimes burn badly.

An ice pack held against the painful cheek may also help because the cold from the ice will help to numb the pain. But don't lie down, otherwise your blood pressure will rise in your head and this will only make the pain worse.

Remember, all the remedies mentioned here will only get rid of the pain for a while. If you have toothache, the best thing you can do is go and see your dentist as soon as possible. Only he will be able to deal with the pain permanently.

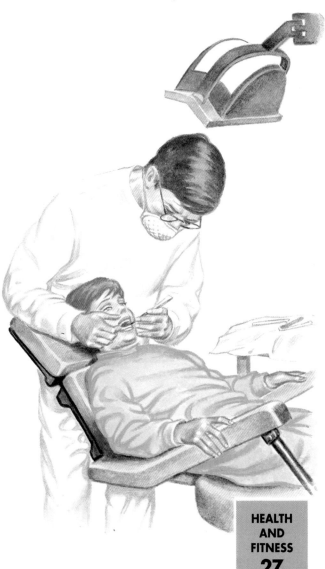

# KEY WORDS

**Alveolus** – a tooth socket. When there's more than one tooth socket, the word is alveoli

**Aspirin** – a widely used pain-killer that contains acetylsalicylic acid

**Calcium salts** – an important element for making the bone structure and teeth in humans and animals

**Canine** – a fang-like tooth for holding on to and tearing tough food like meat

**Caries** – tooth decay: the destruction of a tooth by food particles which produce acids that soften the enamel and allow bacteria to enter the tooth

**Crown** – the part of the tooth that you can see

**Dentine** – the yellowish layer that forms the main part of the tooth

**Diastema** – the gap, or toothless area, in teeth of plant-eaters. Meat eaters have canines instead, which plant-eaters don't need

**Enamel** – the tough outer covering of the crown of the tooth

**Exognathism** – when the lower jaw sticks out more than the upper jaw

**Incisor** – a 'chopping' tooth at the front of the mouth

**Molar/premolar** – a 'grinding' tooth at the back of the mouth

**Ossein** – an organic bone substance

**Plaque** – a film made up of bacteria and food particles. Plaque build-up encourages the development of caries

**Wisdom teeth** – the four molars at the back of the mouth which come out when you are quite old (and supposedly wise!)

# HOW MY BODY WORKS

**HOW MY BODY WORKS** is an educational series that builds into a complete encyclopedia of the human body. Each volume introduces and explains one of its mysteries.

**In Part 16 of How My Body Works**, you've discovered why you need to keep your teeth in good condition.

**PART 17** looks at the origins of life and asks where we came from

### READ ALL ABOUT:
● **How life began** from the formation of our planet to primitive forms of life
● **Human cells** and DNA and what they consist of
● **Early man** – how he lived and fought and how his intelligence evolved

Albert Barillé (pictured left) is the author of this fascinating series of books. The human body is a series of complex systems and mechanisms, so to make it easier for you to understand how the body works, Barillé created The Professor, Captain Courageous, Globus, Toxicus and Virulus, plus many other colourful cartoon characters, to show you around. The Professor and his friends guide you through the body, explaining how it works in a clear and simple way that makes it fun.

# TEST YOUR KNOWLEDGE

**Now you've learned all about teeth, test your knowledge with the *How My Body Works* multiple-choice quiz.**

**1.** What's the name of the tissue that fixes the roots of your teeth in place?
**a)** glue
**b)** cementum
**c)** a tooth socket

**2.** How many teeth do you have?
**a)** 20
**b)** 32
**c)** 28

**3.** What do you call the part of the tooth you can see?
**a)** the crown
**b)** the root
**c)** the pulp cavity

**4.** Which teeth do you use to grind and mash your food?
**a)** incisors
**b)** canines
**c)** premolars and molars

**5.** How many roots do canines have?
**a)** one
**b)** two
**c)** three

**6.** Which part of your tooth grows first?
**a)** the root
**b)** the crown
**c)** the enamel

**7** What is the toothless area that plant-eaters have instead of their canines?
**a)** a gap
**b)** the alveolus
**c)** the diastema

**8.** If you have no wisdom teeth, are you
**a)** stupid
**b)** unlucky
**c)** perfectly normal – but perhaps too young

**9.** What sort of teeth are the elephant's tusks?
**a)** incisors
**b)** wisdom teeth
**c)** canines

**10.** How many incisors do your milk teeth have?
**a)** 4
**b)** 8
**c)** 12

**11.** What's another word for caries?
**a)** tooth decay
**b)** plaque
**c)** bacteria

**12.** What should you make sure your toothpaste contains?
**a)** fluoride
**b)** ossein
**c)** calcium

ANSWERS to the **'How My Body Works'** teeth quiz in issue 17.

**Answers to issue 15:** 1 (c), 2 (c), 3 (all three), 4 (a), 5 (b), 6 (b), 7 (b), 8 (c), 9 (c), 10 (a), 11 (c) 12 (b).

Published by
ORBIS PUBLISHING,
Griffin House,
161 Hammersmith Road,
London W6 8SD

BACK ISSUES
Back issues can be obtained by placing an order with your newsagent or, in case of difficulty, from our back numbers department. All cheques/postal orders should be made payable to Orbis Publishing Ltd.

BACK ISSUE CHARGES
Volume 1:
UK: 99p plus £1.00 p&p;
Eire: IR£0.99 plus £1.00 p&p
Thereafter:
UK: £2.99 plus 50p p&p;
Eire: IR£3.50 plus 50p p&p

ADDRESS FOR
BACK ISSUES:
Orbis Publishing Ltd, Unit 10, Wheel Lane Business Park, Wheel Lane, Westfield, Hastings, East Sussex, TN35 4SG. Tel: 0424 755755

BACK ISSUES OVERSEAS
Please place requests for copies of back issues with your newsagent or, in case of difficulty, please write to the relevant address given:

Australia
Gordon and Gotch Ltd, PO Box 290, Burwood VIC 3125 (Enclose cover price plus $1 p&h per issue)

New Zealand
Gordon and Gotch (NZ) Ltd, PO Box 584, Auckland.
Malta, Singapore & South Africa Back numbers are available at cover price from your newsagent.

© Procidis Albert Barillé
© 1993 Orbis Publishing Ltd, London
N16 93 04 15
Printed in Italy
by Officine Grafiche De Agostini, Novara